CONNECT BIBLE STUDIES

His Dark Materials

Philip Pullman (Scholastic)

Authority
The Fall
Truth
The Future

www.connectbiblestudies.com

connect

linking the Word to the world

CONNECT BIBLE STUDIES: His Dark Materials

Published in this format by Scripture Union, 207-209 Queensway, Bletchley, MK2 2EB, England
Email: info@scriptureunion.org.uk Internet: www.scriptureunion.org.uk

Scripture Union is an international Christian charity working with churches in more than 130 countries providing resources to bring the good news about Jesus Christ to children, young people and families — and to encourage them to develop spiritually through the Bible and prayer.

As well as a network of volunteers, staff and associates who run holidays, church-based events and school Christian groups, Scripture Union produces a wide range of publications and supports those who use the resources through training programmes.

©Damaris Trust, PO Box 200, Southampton, SO17 2DL
Email: office@damaris.org Internet: www.damaris.org

Damaris Trust enables people to relate Christian faith and contemporary culture. It helps them to think about the issues within society from a Christian perspective and to explore God's truth as it is revealed in the Bible. Damaris provides resources via the Internet, workshops, publications and products.

ALSO AVAILABLE AS AN ELECTRONIC DOWNLOAD: www.connectbiblestudies.com

Chief editor: Nick Pollard
Consultant Editor: Andrew Clark
Managing Editor: Di Archer
Written by Di Archer, Caroline Puntis, Tony Watkins

First published 2002
ISBN 1 85999 714 7

British Library Cataloguing-in-Publication Data: a catalogue record for this book is available from the British Library.

Cover design and print production by:
CPO, Garcia Estate, Canterbury Road, Worthing, West Sussex BN13 1BW
Email: connect@cpo.org.uk Internet: www.cpo-online.org

CPO is a Christian publishing charity working in partnership with over 30,000 churches and other Christian organisations worldwide, using the power of design and print to convey the message of Jesus Christ. Established for over 45 years, CPO is the UK's premier supplier of publicity and related resources to the UK church, available through a direct mail catalogue service, an e-commerce web site and most Christian bookshops.

Covers of *Northern Lights, The Subtle Knife* and *The Amber Spyglass* reproduced by kind permission of Scholastic Ltd, 1-19 New Oxford Street, London WC1A 1NU.

Other titles in this series:

Harry Potter and the Goblet of Fire ISBN 1 85999 578 0
The Matrix ISBN 1 85999 579 9
U2: All that you can't leave behind ISBN 1 85999 580 2
Billy Elliot ISBN 1 85999 581 0
Chocolat ISBN 1 85999 608 6
Game Shows ISBN 1 85999 609 4
How to be Good ISBN 1 85999 610 8
Destiny's Child: Survivor ISBN 1 85999 613 2

AI (Artificial Intelligence) ISBN 1 85999 626 4
The Lord of the Rings ISBN 1 85999 634 5
The Simpsons ISBN 1 85999 529 2
Iris ISBN 1 85999 669 8
Dido: No Angel ISBN 1 85999 679 5
Sven-Göran Eriksson: On Football ISBN 1 85999 690 6
Superheroes ISBN 1 85999 702 3

And more titles following — check www.connectbiblestudies.com for latest titles or ask at any good Christian bookshop.

Using Connect Bible Studies

What Are These Studies?

These innovative home group Bible studies have two aims. Firstly, we design them to enable group members to dig into their Bibles and get to know them better. Secondly, we aim to help members to think through topical issues in a Biblical way. Hence the studies are based on a current popular book or film etc. The issues raised by these are the subjects for the Bible studies.

We do not envisage that all members will always be able to watch the films or read the books, or indeed that they will always want to. A summary is always provided. However, our vision is that knowing about these films and books empowers Christians to engage with friends and colleagues about them. Addressing issues from a Biblical perspective gives Christians confidence that they know what they think, and can bring a distinctive angle to bear in conversations.

The studies are produced in sets of four — i.e. four weeks' worth of group Bible Study material. These are available in print published by Scripture Union from your local Christian bookshop, or via the Internet at www.connectbiblestudies.com. Anyone can sign up for a free monthly email newsletter that announces the new studies and provides other information (sign up on the Connect Bible Studies website at www.connectbiblestudies.com/uk/register).

How Do I Use Them?

We design the studies to stimulate creative thought and discussion within a Biblical context. Each section therefore has a range of questions or options from which you as leader may choose in order to tailor the study to your group's needs and desires. Different approaches may appeal at different times, so the studies aim to supply lots of choice. Whilst adhering to the main aim of corporate Bible study, some types of questions may enable this for your group better than others — so take your pick.

Group members should be supplied with the appropriate sheet that they can fill in, each one also showing the relevant summary.

Leader's notes contain:

1. Opening Questions

These help your group settle in to discussion, whilst introducing the topics. They may be straightforward, personal or creative, but are aiming to provoke a response.

2. Summary

We suggest the summary of the book or film will follow now, read aloud if necessary. There may well be reactions that group members want to express even before getting on to the week's issue.

3. Key Issue

Again, either read from the leader's notes, or summarised.

4. Bible Study

Lots of choice here. Choose as appropriate to suit your group — get digging into the Bible. Background reading and texts for further help and study are suggested, but please use the material provided to inspire your group to explore their Bibles as much as possible. A concordance might be a handy standby for looking things up. A commentary could be useful too, such as the *New Bible Commentary 21st Century Edition* (IVP, 1994). The idea is to help people to engage with the truth of God's word, wrestling with it if necessary but making it their own.

Don't plan to work through every question here. Within each section the two questions explore roughly the same ground but from different angles or in different ways. Our advice is to take one question from each section. The questions are open-ended so each ought to yield good discussion — though of course any discussion in a Bible study may need prompting to go a little further.

5. Implications

Here the aim is to tie together the perspectives gained through Bible study and the impact of the book or film. The implications may be personal, a change in worldview, or new ideas for relating to non-churchgoers. Choose questions that adapt to the flow of the discussion.

6. Prayer

Leave time for it! We suggest a time of open prayer, or praying in pairs if the group would prefer. Encourage your members to focus on issues from your study that had a particular impact on them. Try different approaches to prayer — light a candle, say a prayer each, write prayers down, play quiet worship music — aim to facilitate everyone to relate to God.

7. Background Reading

You will find links to some background reading on the Connect Bible Studies website: www.connectbiblestudies.com/

8. Online Discussion

You can discuss the studies online with others on the Connect Bible Studies website at www.connectbiblestudies.com/discuss/

Page numbers quoted throughout are taken from the following paperback editions:
Northern Lights , 1998, The Subtle Knife, 1998, The Amber Spyglass, 2001.
Please note that references may not be an exact match if you are using other editions.

His Dark Materials

Philip Pullman (Scholastic)

Part One: Authority

Well, where is God, if he's alive?
And why doesn't he speak any more?
Mrs Coulter, *The Amber Spyglass*, p. 344

Please read Using Connect Bible Studies *before leading a Bible study using this material.*

Opening Questions

Choose one of these questions.

What do you like or dislike about *His Dark Materials?*	Why do people rebel against authority?
Who or what holds the greatest authority in this country? Why?	Is authority good or bad? Why?

Summary

Authority is an important element in Lyra's early life, growing up within an Oxford college under the care of the Master and various college staff. But Lyra spends as much time as possible roaming free over the college roofs and in the town where she and her friends enjoy fighting with the 'gyptians' from the narrow boats. The college scholars also tread a careful line between respect for authority and freedom, since they live in a world in which the church rules society with an iron grip.

When the Master releases her into the care of the beautiful, charismatic Mrs Coulter, Lyra is both excited and full of trepidation. However, when she discovers that Mrs Coulter is behind the recent disappearance of children around the country, Lyra runs away and ends up in the care of a gyptian family, the Costas. She travels with them to a gathering of gyptian families where she meets the lord of the gyptians, John Faa. Lyra sees in him the same innate authority as both the Master and Lord Asriel, the man she believes to be her uncle.

Lyra joins the gyptians on a journey to the Arctic to rescue the missing children. She also hopes to find Lord Asriel, currently imprisoned because of his heretical investigations into Dust (mysterious charged particles that the Church equates with original sin). Lyra eventually learns that he is preparing to launch an attack on The Authority, God himself. It transpires that The Authority is not the Creator, but merely the first angel. He deceived and enslaved all those who came after him. Instead of a Kingdom of Heaven in which The Authority controls people through the Church, Lord Asriel intends to establish a Republic of Heaven in which everyone is a free citizen.

Key Issue: Authority

Pullman may have won awards with the trilogy *His Dark Materials* (including the Carnegie Medal for *Northern Lights* and the Whitbread Prize for *The Amber Spyglass*), but he certainly stirred up a storm while doing so. Letters to national newspapers have revealed strong reactions from those who love his writings, and those who are disturbed by them. Christians have tended to fall into either or both camps at once — admiring Pullman's incredible imagination and ability to write a ripping yarn, while worrying about his attempts to demote and ultimately destroy God. We begin our study by looking at the issue of authority in the books. Pullman's dethroned God turns out to be ancient and decrepit — how does the Bible describe God? He views the church as a political, manipulative tyranny — what would the Bible say about that? Is it true, therefore, that authority figures are to be spurned? Will knowledge of the world — or worlds — around us prove to be the answer?

Bible Study

Choose one question from each section.

1.   God

The Authority, God, the Creator, the Lord, Yahweh, El, Adonai, the King, the Father, the Almighty — those were all names he gave himself. He was never the creator. He was an angel like ourselves — the first angel, true, the most powerful, but he was formed of Dust as we are ... (Balthamos, *The Amber Spyglass*, p. 33)

   ◆   Read Isaiah 40:6–31. According to Isaiah, what does the authority of God mean? What are the implications for our lives?

   ◆   Read 1 Chronicles 29:10–13; Romans 11:33–36 and 1 Timothy 1:17. What aspects of God's authority do these verses convey? In 1 Timothy 6:11–16, how is God's authority central?

2.   Church

Sisters, let me tell you what is happening, and who it is that we must fight. For there is a war coming. I don't know who will join with us, but I know whom we must fight. It is the Magisterium, the church. For all its history — and that's not long by our lives, but it's many, many of theirs — it's tried to suppress and control every natural impulse. And when it can't control them, it cuts them out ... That is what the church

does, and every church is the same: control, destroy, obliterate every good feeling. So if a war comes, and the church is on one side of it, we must be on the other, no matter what strange allies we find ourselves bound to.'
(Ruta Skadi, *The Subtle Knife,* p. 52)

♦ Read Romans 13:1–5. Why has God established governing authorities? How should the relationship work between those in and under authority?

♦ Read Ephesians 3:7–13. What is the church for? What does it mean to be part of the church?

3. Freedom from authority

Mrs Coulter, I am a king, but it's my proudest task to join Lord Asriel in setting up a world where there are no kingdoms at all. No kings, no bishops, no priests. The kingdom of heaven has been known by that name since the Authority first set himself above the rest of the angels. And we want no part of it. This world is different. We intend to be free citizens of the republic of heaven.
(King Ogunwe, *The Amber Spyglass,* p. 222)

♦ Read Psalm 2:1–12. What attitudes to God's authority are seen in this psalm? What is in store for those who hold these attitudes and why?

Leaders: While this psalm celebrates the crowning of Davidic kings, the New Testament sees that it also talks about the Messiah to come. It is one of the psalms most quoted in the New Testament (e.g. Hebrews 1:3).

♦ Read Luke 20:1–19. Why did the tenants kill the son? How are the priests and teachers an illustration of the parable?

Leaders: Jesus was referring to the Jews' spiritual inheritance being given to others because of the way they treated him.

4. Knowledge

When it was possible to have a belief about God and heaven, it represented something we all desired. It had a profound meaning in human life. But when it no longer became possible to believe, a lot of people felt despair. What was the meaning of life? (Philip Pullman, *The Guardian,* 3 June 2002)

♦ Read Ecclesiastes 1:12–18. What did the Teacher learn from his studies? Why does he come to such a pessimistic conclusion?

♦ Read 1 Corinthians 13:8–13. Regarding knowledge, how does verse 12 goes one step further than verse 8? In what way does love make the difference?

Implications

By what right are you leading us? You are only children! Who gave you the authority?
(The dead, *The Amber Spyglass,* p.375)

Choose one or more of the following questions.

♦ Are there authority figures or organisations to which we struggle to submit? Why? What can we do about it?

♦ Are there ways in which you see the church as manipulative and controlling in the way that Philip Pullman does? What kind of authority do you think the church should have?

♦ Are there limits to our submission to governing authorities? Why or why not?

♦ Are there consequences for not accepting God's authority in all areas of your life? What are they?

♦ What would you say to a Christian friend who will not let their child read *His Dark Materials* because of Pullman's attacks on the concept of God?

♦ How would you respond to someone who agrees with Philip Pullman that God and the church restrict human freedom?

♦ Who knows best — you or God? How do others see God's authority at work in your life?

♦ How important is the pursuit of knowledge? How far can it lead us?

Prayer

Spend some time praying through these issues.

Background Reading

You will find links to some background reading on the Connect Bible Studies website: www.connectbiblestudies.com/uk/catalogue/0016/background.htm

Discuss

Discuss this study in the online discussion forums at www.connectbiblestudies.com/discuss

Members' Sheet: His Dark Materials — Part One

Summary

Authority is an important element in Lyra's early life, growing up within an Oxford college under the care of the Master and various college staff. But Lyra spends as much time as possible roaming free over the college roofs and in the town where she and her friends enjoy fighting with the 'gyptians' from the narrow boats. The college scholars also tread a careful line between respect for authority and freedom, since they live in a world in which the church rules society with an iron grip.

When the Master releases her into the care of the beautiful, charismatic Mrs Coulter, Lyra is both excited and full of trepidation. However, when she discovers that Mrs Coulter is behind the recent disappearance of children around the country, Lyra runs away and ends up in the care of a gyptian family, the Costas. She travels with them to a gathering of gyptian families where she meets the lord of the gyptians, John Faa. Lyra sees in him the same innate authority as both the Master and Lord Asriel, the man she believes to be her uncle.

Lyra joins the gyptians on a journey to the Arctic to rescue the missing children. She also hopes to find Lord Asriel, currently imprisoned because of his heretical investigations into Dust (mysterious charged particles that the Church equates with original sin). Lyra eventually learns that he is preparing to launch an attack on The Authority, God himself. It transpires that The Authority is not the Creator, but merely the first angel. He deceived and enslaved all those who came after him. Instead of a Kingdom of Heaven in which The Authority controls people through the Church, Lord Asriel intends to establish a Republic of Heaven in which everyone is a free citizen.

Key Issue

Bible Study notes

Implications

Prayer

Discuss this with others on the Connect Bible Studies website: www.connectbiblestudies.com

www.connectbiblestudies.com

connect
linking the Word to the world

His Dark Materials

Philip Pullman (Scolastic)

Part Two: The Fall

The child, then, is in the position of Eve, the wife of Adam, the mother of us all, and the cause of all sin ... if it comes about that the child is tempted, as Eve was, then she is likely to fall. On the outcome will depend ... everything. And if this temptation does take place, and if the child gives in, then Dust and sin will triumph.
Fra Pavel, church advisor, *The Amber Spyglass*, p. 71

Please read Using Connect Bible Studies *before leading a Bible study using this material.*

Opening Questions

Choose one of these questions.

Whose fault was the Fall — Adam's or Eve's? Why?	At what age do children begin to sin?
What is 'original sin'?	Why is sin attractive?

Summary

In another world, parallel to ours, everyone has a dæmon[1] — an external soul in the form of an animal. During childhood, dæmons can change into many different animals, but at adolescence a dæmon's form becomes fixed. In this other world, the Reformation never happened and the Church has absolute control. But experimental theologians (scientists) have discovered some mysterious particles, which they call Dust. It is attracted to adults with settled dæmons, but not to children. The Church concludes that Dust is the physical evidence for original sin, and starts a programme of separating children from their dæmons in the hope of preventing them from becoming sinful.

---

[1] Note that *dæmons* are not *demons;* the word in Greek refers to a companion spirit, neither good nor bad.

A young girl named Lyra gets caught up in the events, and concludes that if the Church believes Dust is bad, it must be good. She sets out to search for its source. She meets a boy from our world, Will, and they end up travelling to the world of the dead in search of Lyra's friend, Roger, and Will's father. They discover that life after death is a prison camp rather than Paradise. So they make a way for the ghosts of those who die to merely pass through the world of the dead before returning to being constituent atoms of the universe.

Meanwhile, the Church learns of a prophecy about Lyra as a second Eve, and discovers that if she is tempted and falls, Dust (and, therefore in their minds, sin) will triumph. They determine to kill her before this happens. But the moment of 'temptation' comes when Mary Malone, a physicist from our world, tells Will and Lyra how she fell in love. This helps them to realise their love for each other and their 'fall' occurs when they express this.

Key Issue: The Fall

Philip Pullman appears to turn the central Christian doctrine of the Fall inside out. His serpent is good — a lapsed nun — and Lyra's giving in to temptation is the key to saving the world. His distortion of the Genesis story is vital to the plot. So what actually happened according to the Bible? Are maturity and wisdom really linked with sexual awareness? How does the Bible define innocence? Is original sin more than an ecclesiastical obsession? What was the real fallout for the physical world and mankind from the Fall?

Bible Study

Choose one question from each section. You may like to stick to the Genesis readings throughout. If not, it might be helpful to read Genesis 3:1–24 as a background to this study.

1.   Physical

The night air filled their lungs, fresh and clean and cool; their eyes took in a canopy of dazzling stars, and the shine of water somewhere below, and here and there groves of great trees, as high as castles, dotting the wide savannah ... Will and Lyra fell exhausted on the dew-laden grass, every nerve in their bodies blessing the sweetness of the good soil, the night air, the stars. (The Amber Spyglass, p. 382)

◆   Read Genesis 1:31, 2:8–14, 2:21–25, 3:7 and 3:18. What difference did the Fall make to the physical world?

◆   Read John 1:1–18. What is Jesus' relationship to God, the world and us? What is wrong with the world?

2.   Innocence

The Satan figure is Mary Malone ... and the temptation is wholly beneficent. She tells her story about how she fell in love ... and when it happens they understand what's

going on and are tempted and they ... fall — but it's a fall into grace, towards wisdom,
not something that leads to sin, death, misery, hell — and Christianity.
(Philip Pullman, *Third Way*, Volume 25 Number 2, April 2002)

♦ Read Genesis 2:25–3:5. In what ways were Adam and Eve innocent before the Fall?

♦ Read Mark 10:13 –15; Luke 10:21. What did Jesus value about little children? What did the disciples learn?

3. Maturity and wisdom

I thought, wasn't it a good thing that Eve did, isn't curiosity a valuable quality?
Shouldn't she be praised for risking this? It wasn't, after all, that she was after money
or gold or anything, she was after knowledge. What could possibly be wrong with
that? (Philip Pullman, transcript of *Encounter* (24 March 2002) on Radio National
website — www.abc.net.au/rn/relig/enc/stories/s510312.htm)

♦ Read Genesis 3:6–13. Philip Pullman says that this is the great moment in human history when men and women embraced maturity and wisdom. What actually happened?

♦ Read Romans 1:18–25. How did people become foolish? What is real wisdom?

4. Separation

The boatman held up his hand. 'Not him,' he said, in a harsh whisper.
'Not who?'
'Not him.' He extended a yellow-grey finger, pointing directly at Pantalaimon, whose
red-brown stoat-form immediately became ermine-white.
'But he is me!' Lyra said.
'If you come, he must stay.'
'But we can't! We'd die!'
'Isn't that what you want?'
And then for the first time Lyra truly realized what she was doing. This was the real
consequence. She stood aghast, trembling, and clutched her dear dæmon so tightly
that he whimpered in pain. (The Amber Spyglass, p. 295)

♦ Read Genesis 3:7–24. What different kinds of separation resulted from the Fall?

♦ Read Ephesians 4:17–24. From what different things were the Gentiles separated? What does coming to know Christ involve?

Leaders: It is a recurrent pattern in the Bible that when someone hardens their heart against God, a point comes at which he confirms their choice and hardens their heart even more.

Implications

Mary turned, spyglass in hand, to see Will and Lyra returning ... They were holding hands, talking together, heads close, oblivious to everything else ... There was no need for the glass; she knew what she would see; they would seem to be made of living gold. They would seem the true image of what human beings always could be, once they had come into their inheritance. The Dust pouring down from the stars had found a living home again, and these children-no-longer-children, saturated with love, were the cause of it all.
(*The Amber Spyglass*, p. 497)

Choose one or more of the following questions.

◆ What holds us back from dependent, childlike faith? How can we change?

◆ How can we grow in true maturity and wisdom?

◆ How would you describe the Fall to a child who had just finished reading *His Dark Materials?*

◆ If we are reconciled to God through Jesus, how can we also be reconciled to the physical world and to other people?

◆ How would you reply to a friend who says, 'Well, we are all basically good underneath, aren't we?'

◆ How would you disagree with Pullman's interpretation of the Fall?

◆ What would you say to a friend who has a 'New Age' understanding of the physical world as something to be worshipped?

Prayer
Spend some time praying through these issues.

Background Reading
You will find links to some background reading on the Connect Bible Studies website: www.connectbiblestudies.com/uk/catalogue/0016/background.htm

Discuss
Discuss this study in the online discussion forums at www.connectbiblestudies.com/discuss

Members' Sheet: His Dark Materials — Part Two

Summary

In another world, parallel to ours, everyone has a dæmon — an external soul in the form of an animal. During childhood, dæmons can change into many different animals, but at adolescence a dæmon's form becomes fixed. In this other world, the Reformation never happened and the Church has absolute control. But experimental theologians (scientists) have discovered some mysterious particles, which they call Dust. It is attracted to adults with settled dæmons, but not to children. The Church concludes that Dust is the physical evidence for original sin, and starts a programme of separating children from their dæmons in the hope of preventing them from becoming sinful.

A young girl named Lyra gets caught up in the events, and concludes that if the Church believes Dust is bad, it must be good. She sets out to search for its source. She meets a boy from our world, Will, and they end up travelling to the world of the dead in search of Lyra's friend, Roger, and Will's father. They discover that life after death is a prison camp rather than Paradise. So they make a way for the ghosts of those who die to merely pass through the world of the dead before returning to being constituent atoms of the universe.

Meanwhile, the Church learns of a prophecy about Lyra as a second Eve, and discovers that if she is tempted and falls, Dust (and, therefore in their minds, sin) will triumph. They determine to kill her before this happens. But the moment of 'temptation' comes when Mary Malone, a physicist from our world, tells Will and Lyra how she fell in love. This helps them to realise their love for each other and their 'fall' occurs when they express this.

Key Issue

Bible Study notes

Implications

Prayer

Discuss this with others on the Connect Bible Studies website: www.connectbiblestudies.com

www.connectbiblestudies.com

connect
linking the Word to the world

His Dark Materials

Philip Pullman (Scholastic)

Part Three: Truth

'Liar! Liar! Liar!'
And it sounded as if her voice was coming from everywhere, and the
word echoed back from the great wall in the fog, muffled and
changed, so that she seemed to be screaming Lyra's name, so that
Lyra *and* **liar** *were one and the same thing.*
The Amber Spyglass, p. 308

Please read Using Connect Bible Studies *before leading a Bible study using this material.*

Opening Questions

Choose one of these questions.

What is wrong with lying?	Is honesty *always* the best policy? Why or why not?
What is the worst lie you have ever told and what were the consequences?	Give an example of a person of integrity and explain your choice.

Summary

Lyra Belacqua has been brought up under the care of the Master of Jordan College, believing her parents to be dead. Much of the time she has lived by her wits in a carefree existence, and has become an accomplished liar. The bewitching Mrs Coulter persuades the Master to allow Lyra to leave Jordan College and join her as her personal assistant. Lyra doesn't discover until much later that Mrs Coulter is actually her mother. Before Lyra leaves, the Master secretly gives her a precious gift — an alethiometer, one of only six ever made. Its function is to tell the truth using a system of symbols and pointers. It normally takes years of studying the books to be able to use the alethiometer, but Lyra can soon read it intuitively. She believes that the Master entrusted it to her to give to the man she thinks is her uncle, Lord Asriel, who is investigating Dust — mysterious particles that the Church believes to be evil.

Lyra has to contend with many scheming, duplicitous people (especially those in authority). But she is helped by many characters with real integrity, not least Iorek Byrnison, the armoured polar bear. Lyra discovers that Lord Asriel is her father and eventually reaches him, along with her friend, Roger. Lord Asriel kills Roger in the process of making a bridge into another world. Lyra concludes that if those who believe Dust is evil do such terrible things, it must actually be a good thing, and she sets out to find its source.

She meets a boy, Will, who is trying to find his father and they search together. This search takes them to the world of the dead. A terrifying encounter with some harpies, the ferocious guardians of the world of the dead, enables Lyra to learn that she is most help to others when she is true to herself and tells truthful stories. Eventually, Lyra discovers a very important truth about herself which saves the world from losing its precious Dust forever.

Key Issue: Truth

In *His Dark Materials*, Lyra lands herself in real trouble because she does not tell the truth. Much of the plot turns on the lies and half-truths the characters tell. Several key players are uncomfortable mixtures of good and bad, confusing Lyra and Will's search for what is really going on. Surely these are not merely fictional traits? Is there anyone who has never lied? Does the Bible tell us how much lying really matters? What value does it set on honesty and integrity? How important is it to know the truth about the world around us?

Bible Study

Choose one question from each section.

1. Lying

> *'You said: come with me, and we'll destroy Dust for ever. You remember saying that? But you didn't mean it. You meant the very opposite, didn't you? I see now. Why didn't you tell me what you were really doing? Why didn't you tell me you were really trying to preserve Dust? You could have told me the truth.'*
> *'I wanted you to come and join me,' he said, his voice hoarse and quiet, 'and I thought you would prefer a lie.'*
> (Mrs Coulter and Lord Asriel, *The Amber Spyglass*, p. 401)

◆   Read 2 Kings 5:1–27. How was Gehazi's sin revealed? What were the differences between Naaman and Gehazi?

Leaders: Naaman probably asked for some earth (verse 17) as it was commonly believed that gods could only be worshipped on the soil of the nation they belonged to. Naaman's master (verse 18) was Ben-Hadad, king of Aram.

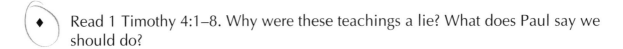 Read 1 Timothy 4:1–8. Why were these teachings a lie? What does Paul say we should do?

2.   Honesty

'Harpies ... When Lyra spoke to you outside the wall, you flew at her. Why did you do that?'
'Lies!' the harpies all cried. 'Lies and fantasies!'
'Yet when she spoke just now, you all listened, every one of you, and you kept silent and still. Again, why was that?'
'Because it was true,' said No-Name. 'Because she spoke the truth. Because it was nourishing. Because it was feeding us. Because we couldn't help it. Because it was true. Because we had no idea that there was anything but wickedness.'
(The Amber Spyglass, p.332)

♦   Read Psalm 15:1–5. What value does God place on honesty? What are the positives and negatives of being honest?

♦   Read Matthew 5:33–37. Why should we keep our promises simple? Why is honesty important?

3. Integrity

Lord Faa, if Iorek Byrnson takes the little girl, she'll be as safe as if she was here with us. All bears are true, but I've known Iorek for years, and nothing under the sky will make him break his word. Give him the charge to take care of her and he'll do it, make no mistake. (Lee Scoresby, *Northern Lights,* p. 207)

♦   Read 1 Samuel 12:1–25. In Samuel's farewell speech, what was important to him about himself and about the people he served? How does God inspire integrity?

♦   Read Titus 2:1–10. What must be taught and why? What is the essence of integrity?

4.   Searching for truth

'Why did you do that?' [Will] shouted. 'Why did you kill him? ... He was my father!'
[The witch] shook her head and whispered, 'No. No! That can't be true. Impossible!'
'You think things have to be possible? Things have to be true! He was my father, and neither of us knew it till the second you killed him! Witch, I wait all my life and come all this way and I find him at last, and you kill him ...' (The Subtle Knife, p. 337)

♦   Read Ecclesiastes 8:1–8, 16, 17; Deuteronomy 29:29. What is 'the explanation of things' (Ecclesiastes 8:1)? How much can we know?

♦   Read John 8:31–47. How did Jesus reason that the Jews hadn't yet found the truth? How is truth related to freedom and belonging?

Implications

But it gradually seemed to me that I'd made myself believe something that wasn't true. I'd made myself believe that I was fine and happy and fulfilled on my own without the love of anyone else. (Mary Malone, *The Amber Spyglass*, p. 466)

Choose one or more of the following questions.

♦ How do we know if we have found the truth about the world?

♦ How can we encourage honesty between one other?

♦ Are there particular situations when you have trouble telling the truth? If so, why, and what can you do about it?

♦ Are 'little white lies' acceptable? Why or why not?

♦ What would you say to someone who declares, 'If God would only show himself, I would believe in him'?

♦ What would you do if your boss asked you to tell a lie at work?

♦ What changes do you need to make to be a person of integrity?

Prayer

Spend some time praying through these issues.

Background Reading

You will find links to some background reading on the Connect Bible Studies website: www.connectbiblestudies.com/uk/catalogue/0016/background.htm

Discuss

Discuss this study in the online discussion forums at www.connectbiblestudies.com/discuss

Members' Sheet: His Dark Materials — Part Three

Summary

Lyra Belacqua has been brought up under the care of the Master of Jordan College, believing her parents to be dead. Much of the time she has lived by her wits in a carefree existence, and has become an accomplished liar. The bewitching Mrs Coulter persuades the Master to allow Lyra to leave Jordan College and join her as her personal assistant. Lyra doesn't discover until much later that Mrs Coulter is actually her mother. Before Lyra leaves, the Master secretly gives her a precious gift — an alethiometer, one of only six ever made. Its function is to tell the truth using a system of symbols and pointers. It normally takes years of studying the books to be able to use the alethiometer, but Lyra can soon read it intuitively. She believes that the Master entrusted it to her to give to the man she thinks is her uncle, Lord Asriel, who is investigating Dust — mysterious particles that the Church believes to be evil.

Lyra has to contend with many scheming, duplicitous people (especially those in authority). But she is helped by many characters with real integrity, not least Iorek Byrnison, the armoured polar bear. Lyra discovers that Lord Asriel is her father and eventually reaches him, along with her friend, Roger. Lord Asriel kills Roger in the process of making a bridge into another world. Lyra concludes that if those who believe Dust is evil do such terrible things, it must actually be a good thing, and she sets out to find its source.

She meets a boy, Will, who is trying to find his father and they search together. This search takes them to the world of the dead. A terrifying encounter with some harpies, the ferocious guardians of the world of the dead, enables Lyra to learn that she is most help to others when she is true to herself and tells truthful stories. Eventually, Lyra discovers a very important truth about herself which saves the world from losing its precious Dust forever.

Key Issue

Bible Study notes

Implications

Prayer

Discuss this with others on the Connect Bible Studies website: www.connectbiblestudies.com

connect

linking the Word to the world

His Dark Materials

Philip Pullman (Scholastic)

Part Four: The Future

Please, remember — the alethiometer does not **forecast;** *it says,* **'If** *certain things come about,* **then** *the consequences will be —'.*
Fra Pavel, church advisor, *The Amber Spyglass,* p. 71

Please read Using Connect Bible Studies *before leading a Bible study using this material.*

Opening Questions

Choose one of these questions.

Why do we want to know what is going to happen in the future?	What is the best thing that could happen to you in the future?
Do you worry about tomorrow, or live for today? Why?	Is *anything* possible? Why or why not?

Summary

When children start to mysteriously disappear, the gyptians plying the rivers in narrow boats are more fearful than most. Being on the margins of society, many of their children have gone missing. Eleven-year-old Lyra is the possessor of an alethiometer — a remarkable instrument which tells her the truth about anything she asks of it — so she joins their expedition to the Arctic to rescue the children. They meet Dr Lanselius, the witches' consul in Lapland, who is very excited when he realises Lyra is the subject of a witches' prophecy. For centuries, they have talked about a girl who is destined to save, not just her own world, but all worlds. However, she can only fulfil her destiny if she is unaware of the task she must accomplish. With the help of the alethiometer, she and the gyptians rescue the children and Lyra sets off to take the alethiometer to her father, Lord Asriel. When she reaches him, he is in the process of making a bridge to another world; he succeeds at the cost of the life of Lyra's friend Roger whom she has recently rescued.

Lyra follows Asriel into the other world in search of mysterious particles called Dust that the Church believes to be evil, but which she has concluded must be both very important and very good. In this other world she meets Will who is searching for his father. He becomes the bearer of a Subtle Knife that can open doors between worlds. However, Lyra is pursued by the church because they have learnt of the witches' prophecy and understand her to be a second Eve who is about to 'fall'. Together Lyra and Will make many tough choices to meet their own objectives, and as they do so they stumble unwittingly onwards to the fulfilment of the prophecy.

Key Issue: The Future

Philip Pullman's characters hear about prophecies and try various means to discover the future: reading the alethiometer or using I Ching, for example. Their fascination with wanting to know the future, both for its own sake, and to help them in their choices, is something many of us can identify with. Horoscopes, fortune-telling, tarot — they are all popular despite our insistence that we are a scientific, logical people. So how does the Bible view prophecy? Where can we turn to when we face difficult choices? Do we live in a 'multiverse' of infinite possible worlds, as Pullman suggests, or does God rule them out? Where will it all end?

Bible Study

Choose one question from each section.

1. Prophecy

There is a curious prophecy about this child: she is destined to bring about the end of destiny. But she must do so without knowing what she is doing, as if it were her nature and not her destiny to do it. If she's told what she must do, it will all fail; death will sweep through all the worlds; it will be the triumph of despair, for ever. The universes will all become nothing more than interlocking machines, blind and empty of thought, feeling, life ... (Serafina Pekkala, *Northern Lights*, p. 310)

◆ Read Deuteronomy 13:1–5 and 1 Corinthians 14:29–33. How is false prophecy identified? What is the purpose of true prophecy?

◆ Read 2 Peter 1:12–2:3. What are the differences between prophecy we can rely on and prophecy we cannot? How did prophecy affect Peter?

2. Choices

Will considered what to do. When you choose one way out of many, all the ways you don't take are snuffed out like candles, as if they'd never existed. At the moment all Will's choices existed at once. But to keep them all in existence meant doing nothing. He had to choose, after all. (The Amber Spyglass, p. 14, 15)

♦ Read 1 Kings 22:1–38. On what basis did Ahab choose his course of action? Why did he make the wrong choice?

♦ Read Acts 1:15–26. Why did the disciples have to make a choice? How and why was Matthias chosen?

3. Possible worlds

They both sat silent on the moss-covered rock, in the slant of sunlight through the old pines, and thought how many tiny chances had conspired to bring them to this place. Each of those chances might have gone a different way. Perhaps in another world, another Will had not seen the window in Sunderland Avenue, and had wandered on tired and lost towards the Midlands until he was caught. (The Subtle Knife, p. 276)

♦ Read Ecclesiastes 3:1–22. How does the writer's view of the future shape his attitude to the present? What is his advice for making the most of life?

♦ Read Colossians 1:9–23. In what ways is Jesus supreme? Why does Paul want the Colossian Christians to understand this?

4. Destiny

You speak of destiny, as if it was fixed. And I ain't sure I like that any more than a war I'm enlisted in without knowing about it. Where's my free will, if you please? And this child seems to me to have more free will than anyone I ever met. Are you telling me that she's just some kind of clockwork toy wound up and set going on a course she can't change? (Lee Scoresby, Northern Lights, p. 309, 310)

♦ Read Isaiah 55:8–13. What does God's sovereignty mean in this passage? What are his intentions?

♦ Read 2 Corinthians 4:1–18. What did Paul see as his ultimate destiny in Christ? How did this perspective affect the way he lived?

Implications

Yes, tell us where we're going! Tell us what to expect! We won't go unless we know what'll happen to us! (The dead, *The Amber Spyglass,* p. 335)

Choose one or more of the following questions.

♦   Are we ever afraid of God speaking to us? Why? What can we do about it?

♦   How do we respond to someone says, 'I think God is saying I should ... '?

♦   Does the church need prophecy today? Why or why not?

♦   How do you make important choices? Could you include God more?

♦   How do we know if we are using time wisely?

♦   How much do you trust God for your future?

♦   Are philosophical discussions about other worlds useful or a waste of time? Why?

♦   What would you say to someone who thinks scientific progress is the answer to the future?

♦   Having looked at the issues raised, would you advise a friend to read *His Dark Materials?* Why or why not?

Prayer

Spend some time praying through these issues.

Background Reading

You will find links to some background reading on the Connect Bible Studies website: www.connectbiblestudies.com/uk/catalogue/0016/background.htm

Discuss

Discuss this study in the online discussion forums at www.connectbiblestudies.com/discuss

Members' Sheet: His Dark Materials — Part Four

Summary

When children start to mysteriously disappear, the gyptians plying the rivers in narrow boats are more fearful than most. Being on the margins of society, many of their children have gone missing. Eleven-year-old Lyra is the possessor of an alethiometer — a remarkable instrument which tells her the truth about anything she asks of it — so she joins their expedition to the Arctic to rescue the children. They meet Dr Lanselius, the witches' consul in Lapland, who is very excited when he realises Lyra is the subject of a witches' prophecy. For centuries, they have talked about a girl who is destined to save, not just her own world, but all worlds. However, she can only fulfil her destiny if she is unaware of the task she must accomplish. With the help of the alethiometer, she and the gyptians rescue the children and Lyra sets off to take the alethiometer to her father, Lord Asriel. When she reaches him, he is in the process of making a bridge to another world; he succeeds at the cost of the life of Lyra's friend Roger whom she has recently rescued.

She follows Asriel into the other world in search of mysterious particles called Dust that the Church believes to be evil, but which she has concluded must be both very important and very good. In this other world she meets Will who is searching for his father. He becomes the bearer of a Subtle Knife that can open doors between worlds. However, Lyra is pursued by the church because they have learnt of the witches' prophecy and understand her to be a second Eve who is about to 'fall'. Together Lyra and Will make many tough choices to meet their own objectives, and as they do so they stumble unwittingly onwards to the fulfilment of the prophecy.

Key Issue

Bible Study notes

Implications

Prayer